KW-054-420

SOME
LOW LEVEL WALKS
IN
STRATHSPEY

Compiled and described by
Ronald A. Laird

The Melven Press

Perth 1986

Published by:
The Melven Press, 176 High Street, Perth, Scotland

© Ronald A. Laird, 1981

Jacket designed by:
Sandy Cheyne

Photographs by:
David Gowans

Maps drawn by:
Carto-Graphic, Edinburgh
Copyright held by John Bartholomew Ltd.

ISBN 0 906664 11 X

Printed by:
Farquhar & Son Ltd., St. Andrew Street, Perth, Scotland

Some Low Level Walks in Strathspey

CONTENTS

Some Low Level Walks in Strathspey

Introduction

As the years go by it is increasingly apparent that more visitors are present in Strathspey to relax and enjoy the refreshingly attractive natural scene. It is equally apparent that a large proportion of these visitors are prepared, even anxious, to participate physically in our natural environment; to become active participants rather than passive watchers. Many wish to escape from the crowds which inevitably accumulate at popular holiday places. It is fortunate that Strathspey is extensive enough, and sufficiently varied, to be able to cope both with the concentration and the dispersal of people.

There are those who, for personal reasons, do not wish to make use of the high level walks on the mountains. This booklet is designed to meet the needs of those who simply wish to walk the countryside and to enjoy the environment and its natural history. Attention must, of course, be drawn to the walks and Nature Trails provided both by the Nature Conservancy Council and the Forestry Commission. The walks described in these pages may be regarded as complementary to those provided by these official bodies, covering areas not included in their activities.

Most of the walks are given a detailed description. Some do not need such descriptions since the environment through which they pass is identical with other walks fully described, and similar features are to be found in each. Broadly the walks are classified into four main groups:

Group A. Those which are circuit routes; that is starting and finishing at approximately the same place.

Group B. Those which are 'there and back' on the same route, or with minor modifications.

Group C. Those which start and finish at separate points, sometimes widely separated.

Group D. Walks provided by one of the official bodies.

Sketch maps are provided. The approximate distances are shown. The time taken is a matter for the walker to determine. Nevertheless, the appropriate O.S. map is almost essential, if only to recognise the prominent features which appear on the route, or to enable the walker to deviate, by personal choice, from the route described. Suitable maps are:— 1in. O.S. Tourist map of Cairngorms.

1:25,000 O.S. Outdoor Leisure Map—High Tops of Cairngorms.

1:50,000 Series O.S.—Kingussie Sheet 35.

1:50,000 Series O.S.—Grantown-on-Spey Sheet 36.

Some Low Level Walks in Strathspey

Precautions to be observed

1. Keep to footpaths, bridle paths, or rights-of-way; thereby causing no, or minimal, disturbance to wild-life, or landowners' interests. Some of these tracks are rights-of-way. Others are simply recognised footpaths over private land. The trespass rules in Scotland are generous. Please respect them.
2. Be sensibly attired for rough tracks and exposed conditions. Start your walk hoping for the best, but prepared for the worst.
3. Act responsibly regarding animal pets you may have with you. If the landowner requires leads to be used, please use them. Otherwise, use discretion, but keep your dog within sight at all times and within controlling range. But note the next precaution.
4. Keep noise down to a level which will not disturb either wild-life or other people.
5. Try and keep tracks and trails free from litter. Even small sweet papers can accumulate into paper trail proportions.
6. The danger and destruction caused by fire can be widespread. Please be sufficiently vigilant not to cause one.
7. The deer-stalking season from August to October may require special precautions to be taken on some of these walks. Please be acquainted with any local requirements in operation.
8. Gates on footpaths are worthy of special mention. A notice requiring a gate to be kept shut means what it says. Otherwise, as a general rule, leave gates as you find them, but please ensure that if you are walking with a party the last person through a gate is sufficiently responsible to observe the rules.

Some Low Level Walks in Strathspey

Summary of Walks

GROUP A. Circuit walks returning to starting point.

No. 1 Inverdruie — Lochan Mhor — Loch-an-Eilein — Returning via the Croft — Black Park — Inverdruie. Distance: 4 miles.

No. 2 Loch-an-Eilein — Einich Gate — Whitewell — Black Park — Loch-an-Eilein. Distance: 7 miles.

No. 3 Coylumbridge — Lairig Ghru track to Iron Bridge — Lochan Deo — track to Coylumbridge. Distance: 6 miles.

No. 4 Coylumbridge — Iron Bridge — Lochan Deo — Loch-an-Eilein — Black Park — Coylumbridge. Distance: 8 miles.

GROUP B. 'There-and-back' on the same track, or with slight modifications.

No. 1 Glen More Car Park — Ryvoan Pass — Strathnethy Bothy (Bynack Stables). Distance: 7½ miles.

No. 2 Coylumbridge/Whitewell/Loch-an-Eilein — Iron Bridge — Lairig Ghru track. Distance: 6/8 miles.

No. 3 Coylumbridge/Whitewell/Loch-an-Eilein — Einich Gate — Glen Einich. Distance: 8/9 miles.

No. 4 Glen Feshie. Tolvah — Estate road right-of-way — Ruighaiteachain (Glen Feshie bothy). Distance: 8½ miles.

No. 5 Kincardine Church — Tulloch Moor — Aundorach. Distance: 6 miles.

No. 6 Kingussie — Ruthven barracks — Ben Bhuidhe — Glentromie Lodge — Bhran Cottage — return to Tromiebridge. Distance: 12 miles (maximum).

GROUP C. Routes starting and finishing at separate points.

No. 1 Loch-an-Eilein/Coylumbridge/Whitewell to Loch Morlich via Iron Bridge. Distance: 5/6 miles.

No. 2 Loch Morlich via the Sluggan to Milton. Distance: 5 miles.

No. 3 Wade's Road from Kinveachy to Sluggan Bridge with deviation to Carrbridge or continue via Inverlaidnan Hill to Little Slochd. Distance: 4/7 miles.

No. 4 Loch-an-Eilein — Loch Gamnha — Inshriach Bothy — Feshiebridge. Distance: 6 miles.

No. 5 Glenmore — Ryvoan Bothy — Forest Lodge — Nethybridge. Distance: 11 miles.

No. 6 Easter-Lynwilg — Allt-na-criche — 'Burmah' Road — Caggan Bridge — Inverlaidnan — Carrbridge (alternative diversion via Wade's Road in reverse direction to Kinveachy). Distance: 11 to 13 miles.

Some Low Level Walks in Strathspey

GROUP D. Walks provided by Official Organisations.

No. 1   Forestry Commission.
- (a) Walks in Glenmore Forest area.
  Details from Forestry Commission Information Centre at Glenmore.
- (b) Rockwood Ponds near Insh on B.970
  (See Route No. B.6).

No. 2   Nature Conservancy Council.
- (a) Craigellachie Birch Wood National Nature Reserve.
- (b) Loch-an-Eilein Nature Trail.

It is not intended to add any description of these walks since that has already been very adequately dealt with by the Official bodies concerned.

Details of these walks may be obtained from the Spey Valley Tourist Organisation information centre, or, where appropriate, the Forestry Commission Information Centre at Glen More.

Some Low Level Walks in Strathspey

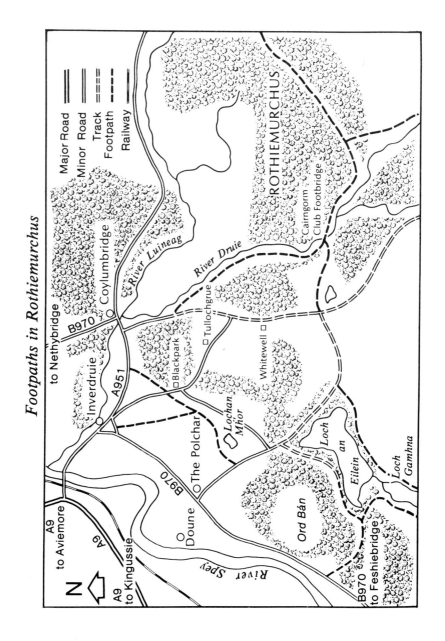

Some Low Level Walks in Strathspey

Description of Walks

GROUP A.

No. 1   Inverdruie — Lochan Mhor — Loch-an-Eilein — returning via
The Croft — Black Park — Inverdruie. Map: Footpaths in
Rothiemurchus.   Distance: 4 miles.

At Inverdruie on the Glenmore Road a triangle of roads is formed at
the junction of the B.970 and the A.951. On the South side of the
triangle there is a gate on to the moorland. Pass through this gate and
observe that you are on an estate private footpath. Follow this track for
about ½ mile when it is joined by another track coming in from the left.
Continue on the combined track and after a short distance Lochan Mhor
will be seen on your left. This attractive lochan, surrounded on three
sides by Birch trees, is a water-fowl sanctuary maintained by the Rothiemurchus estate. The Little Grebe, Tufted Duck, the Mallard and other
species may be seen during the breeding season. The scattered old Pine
trees are well used by Crossbills, whilst in the Autumn flocks of Redpolls
will be seen actively feeding on the Birches. Continue along the track
through heather moorland with scattered Pines and Birches and having
passed a cottage on your right and another on the left you will reach a
minor public road. Turn left and follow the road for about ½ mile until
you reach Loch-an-Eilein. Here the Nature Conservancy Council have
provided a Nature Trail walk, of about 3 miles distance, around the loch.
See Group D.
For the return journey, continue down the public road from the car
park for a short distance. A rough road leads off to the right. Follow this
road passing some handsome Larch trees on your left. Soon you will come
to farm pasture land. There may be cattle grazing, but look out for Roe
Deer grazing there too, particularly where the meadows meet the Birches.
A large house, the Croft, and a cottage are passed on your right. Another
large house, Monadh Liadh, appears among the trees on your left. Now
there are Birch trees with some Juniper on both sides of the road. Shortly,
another white cottage, Black Park, appears on your left, and here you
join a public road which has come downhill from the right from Whitewell.
Follow the road, a quiet road, with open moorland and Pines on each
side, and after ½ mile you join the A.951 at Inverdruie.

9

Some Low Level Walks in Strathspey

No. 2 Loch-an-Eilein – Einich Gate (Lochan Deo) – Whitewell – Black
Park – Loch-an-Eilein.
Map: Footpaths in Rothiemurchus. Distance: 7 miles.

From the entrance to Loch-an-Eilein car park take the gated road
through the Pines on the East side of the loch. This road forms part of
the nature trail provided by the Nature Conservancy Council and passes
through woods of old Pine Trees with some Birches at first. Pass Forest
Cottage and continue on through the gate into the National Nature Conservancy Reserve. Half a mile or so further on, and having crossed a burn,
your track branches to the left, the nature trail continuing to the right.
At this stage you have left the close canopy forest behind and now the
track continues gently uphill over open heather moorland with scattered
Pines of varying ages. This moorland was formerly forested but fellings
during the two world wars soon reduced it to the state in which you see
it today. However, as you walk along the track you will notice young
Pine Trees, naturally regenerated, emerging from the rank heather. In
August the heather (Ling) is in full bloom. The moorland and hill-side is
a vast mass of purple. The deep blue blaeberry may be picked at the
trackside at the end of July. The isolated Pine trees are worth examining
for Crested Tits and the busy cone-stripping Crossbills. The track crosses
two burns which come down from the hillside, Coire Buidhe, on the right.
Observe the crystal clear quality of the water. Further up the track a bank
of sand and gravel is exposed. You will see more of this feature on other
walks in the area. This illustrates the work of the glaciers about 10,000
years ago which eroded the mountains, created the glens, and eventually
deposited the eroded material over Strathspey in general, and Rothiemurchus in particular.

Where the path divides, take the right branch. The White House on the
hillside is Achnagoichan, formerly a croft. A short distance ahead you
reach Lochan Deo. The locked gate is the Einich Gate, leading to the glen
and loch of that name. The lochan, as you can see, is another of these
quiet and peaceful places in which the area abounds. The forest on the right
is a good example of natural Caledonian Pine Forest. Perhaps you may see
the Roe Deer here. The well-defined, but narrow, tracks through the
heather are the paths which the Red Deer follow on their evening journeys
from the hill to the richer feeding lower down. Crossbills, Crested Tits
and, in the summer, Meadow and Tree Pipits are to be seen here. The high-
pitched musical jingle of the Gold-crest is a normal feature of the old Pine
woods, where it is often joined by the Coal-tit. Observe on the left by the

Some Low Level Walks in Strathspey

gate the Bear-berry plants, the low, prostrate, ground-hugging evergreen whose fruit appears in late summer. The scarred appearance of the moorland in the immediate vicinity of the gate, and to the North, is the result of water pipe laying operations. Loch Einich is the principal water supply for the area. Nature, in not too many years will heal the scars. The heather will slowly eliminate all signs of them.

At this point your return journey begins. Leave the Lochan on your right and, walking Northwards, follow the track. You will soon see a sign-post pointing to Coylumbridge. There are young natural Pines on your right and heather moorland on your left. The cottages at Whitewell will now appear on the hillside on your left, and having passed through two gates continue a short distance beyond the scrub trees and follow any of the narrow tracks uphill over the dry heather moorland. Here you will see a cairn which is a memorial to two unfortunate climbers who lost their lives in January 1928 on Braeriach. It is, as the inscription tells, the burial place of one of them. A few yards uphill and to the West of the cairn you will join a public road. Turn right and follow this road. Between Whitewell and the cattle grid, a distance of ½ mile, the panoramic view from the North-West, through East to South-West, is magnificent, from the Monadh Liadh range of mountains right round the sky line to Cairngorm, Ben Macdui, the great cut made by the Lairig Ghru, with the mass of Braeriach between it and Glen Einich, followed by Carn ban Mor.

To the North can be seen Loch Pityoulish nestling between the Birch covered low hills, and sweeping the eyes round the middle foreground one covers the extent of the natural native Pinewoods of Rothiemurchus. In the background one sees the Kincardine Hills with the well-ordered Forestry Commission plantations on their lower slopes. This is by far the most rewarding 'low-level' view point in the area.

The moorland on both sides of the public road here produces an interesting botanical array during June and July in particular. Close by the roadside may be seen the Mountain Everlasting, a low whitish flower with small woolly hairy leaves. Two flowers with similar names – the Chickweed Wintergreen and the Common Wintergreen grow on this moorland. The similarity ends with their names, for in appearance they are totally different as any wild flower guide will show.

Now follow the public road, over the cattle grid, through Upper Tullochgrue farm, and downhill through the Birchwoods to the road junction at Black Park. Turn left for Loch-an-Eilein or right for Inverdruie and Aviemore.

Some Low Level Walks in Strathspey

No. 3 Coylumbridge — Lairig Ghru track to Iron Bridge — return via Lochan Deo — Coylumbridge.
Map: Footpaths in Rothiemurchus. Distance: 6 miles.

On the South side of the A.951 at Coylumbridge a track is sign-posted to Lairig Ghru and Braemar. Start off your journey by following this track through the forest, a well-defined rough road at the beginning. Having passed Lairig Ghru Cottage on your left continue until a signpost near a cairn of boulders indicates that your track branches off to the left. Here the woodland is mainly Birch with patches of Juniper here and there. Examine the Juniper; squeeze one of the berries and what to some may be a familiar smell will result. Siskins, amongst the other woodland birds, may be seen here on the more open trees. The Tree-creeper will be seen by the very observant.

The track continues over fairly open tree-studded ground with the rush of the River Druidh on your left. A short distance ahead, and in more dense Pines, a gate takes the track into the National Nature Reserve. At first the forest is dense. Then it becomes more open and the ground is quite boggy. In fact, in winter this track is often the bed of a stream. Mid-summer sees the area well covered with Cotton-grass.

The typical heather is the Cross-leaved Heath, flowering in July, and very much at home in boggy conditions. Roe Deer are sometimes seen in the clearings over on the right.

Now the track passes alongside the river and the natural Pine forest. Capercaillies frequent these trees where, if disturbance is kept to a minimum, they may be seen in the tree tops. Shortly the track opens out, passing over fairly open heather moorland and soon it is joined by another track converging from the right. A short distance ahead is the Iron Bridge, the Cairngorm Club footbridge, over the Allt Druidh. The river rushes down from the Lairig Ghru and has been joined by the Am Bennaidh which starts its life in the Coire Bennaidh on the north side of Braeriach. See walk No. B.3. The junction point of the two burns is just up stream from the bridge. Walks beyond the bridge are described in B.2 and C.1. Again the forest here is native Pinewood. There is another memorial cairn among the heather and Pines on the down-stream side of the bridge. The inscription on its conveys its purpose.

The return journey begins by taking the other well-marked track which joined your original track a short distance downstream. Continuing westwards for about a mile with rather boggy natural forest on your left Lochan Deo will again come into sight. The track is rather gravelly and dry in places. Notice the very prostrate Bearberry in such situations.

Some Low Level Walks in Strathspey

Blaeberry and Cowberry are abundant. In the boggy patches by the trackside observe, in June especially, the display of Butterwort with its rosette of bright green ground-hugging leaves. Bog Asphodel, with its yellow spike, takes its place later in the summer. Bird's Foot Trefoil is the other yellow track-side flower prominent throughout the early summer.

The lochan and its surroundings were described in walk A.2, but look out for the pair of Oystercatchers which habitually nest there every summer and the Mallard duck which accompanies them. Moorland waders use the lochan shores early on Summer mornings. A walk by this lochan and its woodland early in the morning during May and June can be very satisfying.

As you approach the gate and the track junction the forest is now young self-regenerated Pines. These, in their younger stages, had been fenced off against the marauding deer. On passing through the gate turn right as the sign-post indicates and a walk of about two miles will take you back to Coylumbridge.

No. 4   Coylumbridge — Iron Bridge — Lochan Deo — Loch-an-Eilein
— Black Park — Coylumbridge.
Map: Footpaths in Rothiemurchus. Distance: 8 miles.

This route has already been substantially covered in walks A.1, A.2, and A.3. Having arrived at Black Park from Loch-an-Eilein continue down the public road to Inverdruie. A short distance down this road, and having passed a Water Board building on the right, there is a gate on the right which gives access to a track leading over the moorland towards Coylumbridge. Follow this track until it joins the main road. Turn right for Coylumbridge.

Some Low Level Walks in Strathspey

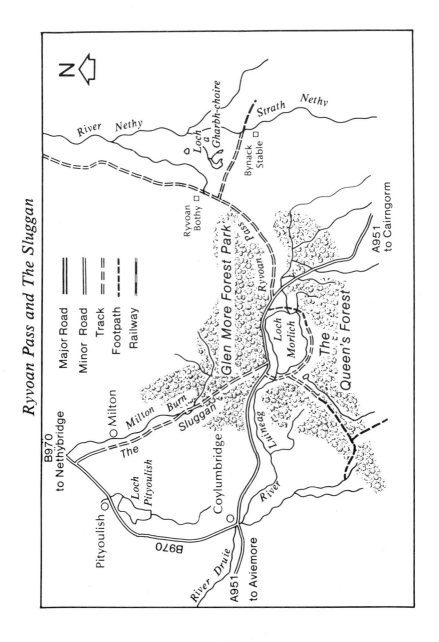

Ryvoan Pass and The Sluggan

Legend:
- Major Road
- Minor Road
- Track
- Footpath
- Railway

River Nethy

Loch a Gharbh-choire

Strath Nethy

Bynack Stable

Ryvoan Bothy

Glen More Forest Park

Ryvoan Pass

A951 to Cairngorm

The Queen's Forest

Loch Morlich

B970 to Nethybridge

Milton

Milton Burn

The Sluggan

Coylumbridge

Luineag

River

Loch Pityoulish

Pityoulish

B970

River Druie

A951 to Aviemore

Some Low Level Walks in Strathspey

GROUP B.

No. 1   Glen More Car Park — Ryvoan Pass — Strathnethy Bothy (Bynack Stables).
Map: Ryvoan Pass. Distance 7½ miles.

On leaving the car park follow the road to the left which leads to and passes Glenmore Lodge. Continue by this track with the Forestry Commission plantation on your left. Shortly you will pass through a gate and cross a burn. Follow up the hill with the plantation now on your right and tree-scattered rough heather moorland on your left. Notice the old Pine stumps, some covered with Blaeberry showing that at one time the moorland was well forested. The track continues uphill, and by the track-side the small, hanging, bell-like flowers of the Wintergreen, rather like Lily of the Valley, may be seen in July.

The Green Lochan, Lochan Uaine, now appears on the right with the steep screes of Creag nan Gall behind it. The depth of the water, and the water-logged tree trunks, contribute to the peculiar colouring of the water. The name Lochan Uaine is given to at least two other lochans in the Cairngorms, one on the North side of Cairn Toul, and the other on the East side of Ben Macdui.

Notice the precarious existence of the Pine trees on the scree slopes. Compare them with the growth on the opposite side of the pass. Naturally regenerated Pines may be seen on the trackside. These seem to have escaped the attention of browsing deer but have difficulty in reaching a respectable height because of the wind which tends to howl through the pass during most of the year. Consequently the trees, although anything but young in appearance, scarcely emerge above the rank heather.

Further up, the track divides. Straight ahead leads to the Ryvoan Bothy and on to the Forest Lodge and through the Abernethy Forest to Nethybridge. Our track branches to the right and continues uphill. Soon the head of the pass is reached and the extent of the Abernethy moorland is seen before you. Heather-surrounded lochans of varying sizes meet the eye. These are sites of Black-headed Gull breeding colonies. Such gulls have long since abandoned the sea and spend most of their lives either well inland for breeding purposes or on the lower, richer farm lands. On the moorland, in May and June, Skylarks, Meadow-pipits, Wheatears and Whinchats are numerous, whilst overhead may be seen the passage of the Peregrine Falcon. Sometimes the Golden Eagle soars high over this moorland. The muddy, marshy

Some Low Level Walks in Strathspey

edges of the numerous lochans are much frequented by waders, Dunlin, Redshank, and Snipe being prominent. Early on a May morning would be a rewarding time to keep these lochans under observation. Here again the various heathers are resplendent, the pinkish Cross-leaved Heath in the boggy places from late June onwards, followed by the rich blue of the Bell-heather in July, then the great masses of Ling, the purple heather, in August. The white patches of Cotton-grass are very much in evidence around the lochan shores in July. The isolated groups of Pines to be seen at random over the moorland represent the remains of the ancient forest which formerly covered this moorland.

Now continue along the track to the Bynack Stables on the turbulent River Nethy. This is the return point on the route but Walk No. A.5 gives an extension downstream to Forest Lodge. Return now by the same route and, as with other 'there-and-back' tracks you will enjoy quite a different scene on the return journey. Particularly so is this the case when descending the Ryvoan Pass.

No. 2 Coylumbridge — Iron Bridge — Lairig Ghru track junction — return.
Map: Rothiemurchus footpaths. Distance: 7/8 miles.

This walk may also be started at Loch-an-Eilein or Whitewell and the earlier stages as far as the Iron Bridge are described in Walks A.3 and A.4.

Having reached the Iron Bridge, or more correctly the Cairngorm Club footbridge, cross the river and follow the track upstream. Shortly the Allt Bennaidh may be seen joining the Allt Druidh after its short, but turbulent journey from Glen Einich. Here you are in the old natural Pine forest. The track continues and, with the Allt Druidh on your right, soon reaches an open meadow. This is rather an unexpected sight, straight from the forest into what has undoubtedly been the scene of much crofting activity in times past. The foundations of buildings, houses, may be seen on both sides of the river, and the ford which gave contact between the two sides. Considering the extent and quality of the foundations these buildings were more substantial than mere hovels or summer sheilings. Rob Roy Macgregor, that notorious yet much revered chieftain of the 17th century Highland scene, has an association with this community. Reflecting into history can be interesting in this, or any other area, since it can depict a scene of tremendous human activity in stark contrast with the derelict scene of today. In this instance history tells us that in the 16th century the Shaws were the holders of Rothiemurchus, but

Some Low Level Walks in Strathspey

Allan Shaw, their Chief, was outlawed for having murdered his step-father. He was dispossessed of the land and the Chief of Grant purchased the right to hold the estate and gave it to his second son, Patrick (1570). There was fairly constant fighting between the Grants and the Shaws who were intent on regaining their land and who had enlisted the help of the Chief of Mackintosh who, in fact, was the Shaw's Chieftain. A hundred years or so later another Patrick Grant, a grandson of the first, was the Laird of Rothiemurchus. He was known as Macalpine, a clan related to the Macgregors with whom he was on very friendly terms. The feud between the Shaws and the Grants showed itself in the actions of The Mackintosh who set up a mill outside the western boundary of Rothie-murchus and announced his intention of diverting water from Rothie-murchus to run the mill. Patrick Grant, otherwise Macalpine, naturally objected. At this the Mackintosh threatened to bring his men into Rothiemurchus and burn the place. Patrick appealed to his friend Rob Roy for help. He duly arrived with his men from Balquidder, a distance of over 100 miles. The Mackintosh was impressed and withdrew, but as a salutary mark Rob Roy burned down the mill. This is said to be the origin of Black Mill at the entrance to Glen Feshie. Rob Roy then returned to Balquidder but left behind two young Macgregors who would act as messengers if the need for further help arose against The Mackintosh. One of these young men ran off with Patrick Grant's daughter, there having been much opposition from her father. To help against enemies was one thing, but to help himself to a daughter was beyond the bounds of friendship, willing though the daughter was. After some years the Laird relented and gave the Macgregor the croft of Allt Druie the ruins of which are now clearly seen. The last Macgregor of Allt Druie died in 1890. As a postscript to the diverting of the water episode it is worth noting the direction in which the water flows in that area today. Walk No. C.4 traverses the moorland between Rothiemurchus and Black Mill via Inshriach. All the major running water flows South towards the River Feshie. This would seem to suggest that the pattern of natural drainage has changed in the past 300 years. Perhaps that is the case. Far better to disturb the course of rivers than to disturb the course of local human history and so deprive us of at least one of its more interesting incidents.

So much for history, but it is many a long year since any human being lived here. Yet the forest has been slow to encroach upon the land which was formerly farmed by the Macgregors. There are trees, though, which must have been known by them. Notice, for instance, the handsome specimens of Birch in the vicinity. One in particular, on the West side of the river, is an outstanding example of the Pendulous Birch whose long

Some Low Level Walks in Strathspey

feathery branches reach down to the ground.

The track now continues again into the forest and gently uphill through the open Pines with much Juniper undergrowth. The Blaeberries here are plentiful and particularly luscious in July. In September the Cowberry, locally referred to as the Cranberry, is well worth picking. In June their white bell-like flowers with shiny tough evergreen leaves make an attractive carpet to the forest. The Crowberry may also be seen on the track-side. It bears its blackish fruit in July. This is an unusual type of plant. The male and female flowers are on separate plants. Hence, although you will find many plants, only a few of them will bear fruit. This same observation also applies to the Junipers. So you will see some with berries and some totally devoid of berries.

The track now continues uphill to the sign-posted junction, referred to locally as Piccadily. Ahead is the track to Loch Morlich. See Walk No. C.1. Uphill to the right is the track leading into the Lairig Ghru. This is a convenient point at which to retrace footsteps and enjoy the changing scene. The sweeping extent of the Monadh Liadh hills lies in front of you in the distance. The long shadows thrown by the late afternoon sun emphasise the numerous rounded glens and streams which intersect these hills, so creating a massive sculptured effect.

No. 3   Coylumbridge/Whitewell/Loch-an-Eilein — Einich Gate — Glen Einich track to last Pine trees.
Map: Rothiemurchus footpaths. Distance: 8/9 miles.

The initial stages of this walk are covered by Walks A.2, 3 and 4. So we shall take up the trail from Einich Gate.

Start from the gate and follow the well-defined track leading uphill in a south-easterly direction. This track has its origins well into the past when the people of Rothiemurchus had summer sheilings at Loch Einich itself. To these well-watered grassy places the stock would be driven up from the crofts and there the summer would be spent. The meagre feeding on the home ground would then be conserved for winter use. Most of the families involved moved up with the stock and lived in what may have been rather primitive, but stone-built, shelters. So the track you are invited to follow has been well used in times past. The present condition of the track is, however, due to the activities of the water pipe laying contractors as mentioned earlier.

The native Caledonian forest is particularly in evidence here on your left. The naturally well-spaced Pines permit light to pass through the canopy and so there develops a rich ground flora, mainly of Blaeberry,

18

Some Low Level Walks in Strathspey

with Ling, Cowberry and Crowberry. The woodland provides shelter for the Red Deer and the Roe Deer, and in its very heart, the Capercaillie. On the right is the heather moorland, boggy in places, with well scattered Pines. Cadha Mor is the hill on your right. Note the richness of the natural tree growth which extends well up the hill-side to close on the 2000 feet contour. In addition to the tree-scattered moorland birdlife mentioned in Walk A.2 such summering birds as Wheatears and Whinchats may be encountered on this walk. The most numerous bird species of the forest is clearly the Chaffinch, but be on the look-out for Siskins, Crossbills and Crested Tits.

Meanwhile the track continues gently uphill. The ground underneath the moorland is all glacial moraine deposits which are quite thick here and represent the terminal moraines from Glen Einich and later moraines from the main ice movement down Strathspey. On top of the morainic deposits peat has accumulated, to a considerable depth in places. You will observe that apart from the scattered Pines still to be seen, tree stumps, or roots, are very much part of the moorland scene. These are the remains of a forest which formerly covered this moorland.

After a mile or so the track divides. The old track drops down to the river, Am Bennaidh. The newer one, the vehicle track, continues up the hill. Take the uphill track which will give views of some of the glen's features. The return track will follow the river when you will see why the new one has been necessary. On reaching the top of the rise Carn Eilrig with its conical head is the prominent feature on your left whilst ahead can be seen the great corries of Braeriach, and, on the right, the great bulk of Sgoran Dhubh. The flat-topped glacial terraces ahead are particularly fascinating features, dominated by the ever-stretching boggy heather moorland. It is not, however, without interest. Shallow peaty lochans appear here and there. These are attractive places for bird-life in the breeding season. Dunlins and Oystercatchers use these lochans. The Meadow Pipit is still the prominent moorland bird in the summer season. You are on the edge of Golden Eagle country here. You may be fortunate in sighting an Eagle elegantly soaring high overhead on the up-rising warmer air currents.

Loch Einich itself is still some miles away up the glen and remains well out of sight at the foot of the massive crags which surround it. Some of these crags are clearly visible. On the right is Sgoran Dhu Mor, the Big Black Peak, with its long face of challenging rock structures continuing into Sgor Gaoith, the Peak of the Winds. On the left the mass of Braeriach dominates the scene with Einich Carn on its right. But that is all climbing country and so outside the scope of this booklet.

Some Low Level Walks in Strathspey

Footpaths in Glen Feshie

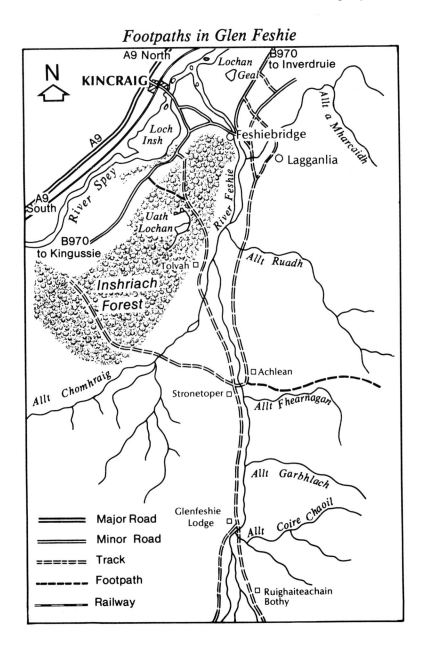

Some Low Level Walks in Strathspey

Our track now drops steeply downhill and joins the river, and here you see the last trees in the glen, a small group of Pines on one side of the river and a single tree on the other. The forest must have been fairly extensive at one time. These trees, in their sheltered hollowed sites, are the sole survivors.

The return track is by the river in its steep-sided gorge. The great scars of the landslips on both banks are prominent. You can well imagine the torrents of water from the melting snows rushing down the gorge, under-cutting the banks and removing the natural support for the heathery peat on the steep sides. The great slip of land is then inevitable. The gorge also provides protection as you can see, for the increasing numbers of Pine trees living very sheltered lives. The ever-bobbing Dipper, with with its white breast patch, is the bird of the river here, even throughout the hardest of winters. It is remarkable how this white breast patch helps to conceal the bird as it stands on a river-side rock, by interrupting its otherwise blackish outline. The Ring Ousel, the Blackbird of the mountains, lives on the hillside screes. Listen for its single-note, repetitive song. The Common Sandpiper may be heard trilling its way up or downstream, particularly where the gorge opens out and the sides are less steep. The Grey Wagtail, prominently yellow despite its name, is another of the riverside birds.

The river soon continues its way into the forest to the point where it joins the Allt Druie from the Lairig Ghru, whilst our track bears on the left and joins the main track. Continue on the main track back down to the Einich Gate where our walk started.

No. 4   Glen Feshie. Tolvah — Estate road Right-of-Way Ruighaiteachain (Glen Feshie bothy).
Map: Glen Feshie. Distance: 8½ miles.

About 1½ miles south-west of Feshiebridge on the B.970 a minor road, sign-posted to Glen Feshie, branches off to the left (South). Follow this road for about 2½ miles, at which point the public road comes to an end. A locked gate across it provides access for authorised vehicles. A side gate enables pedestrians to pass through. The road is private but at the same time part of the public footpath right-of-way to Deeside via Glen Geldie.

The walk starts at this point. The first mile is through young forestry plantation which tends to restrict the outward view on either side. It soon opens out. Meanwhile you will have noticed the rich carpet of Bearberry on each side of the road, the typical plant of sandy, dry conditions. The

Some Low Level Walks in Strathspey

yellow Bird's-foot Trefoil often grows with it. In places the Bearberry is even attempting to creep on to the road. You will also have noticed on the east side of the glen the Pine growth on the screes of Creag Leathan, a continuation of what will be seen again on the Inshriach walk (C.4).

Having passed on your right the Scottish Rights-of-Way Society's sign-posted track to Tromie Bridge you will arrive at Stronetoper, a wayside white cottage which was formerly the school for the children of the crofts in the glen. As a school it was closed in 1952. The depopulating process had taken its toll of the families. At one time in the glen there may have been at least eight crofts, two of which can be seen on the east side of the river, Achlean still in use, and Achleum, still standing, but long since empty as a croft.

At Stronetoper you pass through the gate which leads on to the Glen Feshie estate. Please observe the conditions requested by the estate on its sign. Shortly above Stronetoper an estate bridge crosses the river. This may be used by walkers. Notice how wide the glen is now becoming, the flat river terraces indicating the former course and level of the river over the glacial moraine deposits. Note the width of the flood plain of the river and the turbulence of the river where it passes over the outcrops of rocks. This general pattern of river course and bed continues for the next mile or so.

You are now entering an area of old natural Pine forest, an open growth of trees with a good mixture of Alders and Birches. The Alders are particularly prominent by the roadside where the river's influence on the wetness of the land is very much felt. The ground vegetation pattern here in Summer and Autumn is very attractive and relatively rich in species. The reason for this is partly to be seen on the other side of the river. There, on the east side, you now look straight into the jaws of the Coire Garbhlach, the Rugged Corrie. Rugged and forbidding it certainly is. Yet at this corrie we have a transition zone between the Granites and the Schists, the newer igneous rocks, and the older, but much altered, sediments. This leads to the exposure of lime-rich rock structures in the corrie cliffs and elsewhere further up the glen where similar geological conditions occur. So in this Coire Garbhlach there is an unusually interesting assemblage of the lime-loving montane flora which is also prominent on the Ben Lawers range in Perthshire. But a venture into the corrie is scarcely a low-level walk. The alluvial soils of the glen bottom have, in places, become enriched by sediments brought down in the hill burns from these calcareous corrie cliffs, and this feature is reflected in the vegetation. Consequently, one is likely to encounter on this walk a floral pattern not seen on other walks.

Some Low Level Walks in Strathspey

Aviemore and the Cairngorms from Craigellachie.   D. Gowans

Some Low Level Walks in Strathspey

Red Deer stag.   D. Gowans

Some Low Level Walks in Strathspey

Loch an Eilein and its castle.   D. Gowans

Some Low Level Walks in Strathspey

River Feshie.   D. Gowans

Some Low Level Walks in Strathspey

To the south of Coire Garbhlach, and on the lower slopes, can be seen the remains of the old forest and the fenced in new plantations, attempts being made to replenish the vanishing tree stock of the glen and restore it to something approaching the original natural condition. Here too is to be seen the Juniper in its very natural environment. In places it is the dominant shrub growth. This is particularly noticeable further up the glen towards the turning point of the walk.

The bird life is typical of the well covered valley bottom. The more profuse, and varied the vegetation, the richer it becomes. The river has its waders, in particular the Oystercatcher, whose piping fills the June morning air. The Common Sandpiper and the Curlew are much in evidence, with the Redshank and Common Snipe here and there. The Dipper and Grey Wagtail are the resident birds of the river side. Skylarks and Meadow Pipits are numerous as summering breeders. The Whinchat, and sometimes the Stonechat, uses the lower scrub vegetation as a song perch. The Wheatear will be seen flying low along the roadside from perch to perch, its white rump being a prominent identifying-feature. The tree-using birds contain the typical range of tits. Later in the summer be observant for the chattering family flights of Long-tailed Tits. Birches, Pines and Alders attract them. This applies also to the Treecreeper, common but often unobserved. It is probably the bird which is least concerned about the presence of human beings in its natural habitat. The Chaffinch is by far the most numerous of the finch species, or any other species too. The handsome cock Siskin prefers his prominent song perch to be on an isolated tree. The summer visiting insectivores, the Willow Warbler, the Redstart, the Spotted Flycatcher, and perhaps the Pied Flycatcher, find the open forest of Glen Feshie very much to their liking. Jackdaws are common users of the glen. Its predatory habits, particularly on the nestlings of the small song birds, are often overlooked. The much persecuted Hooded Crow, with its hybrid versions resulting from inter-breeding with the Carrion Crow, is always around the area. Overhead the Raven may be seen croaking its way between the higher cliffs and the higher hillsides. You are on the edge of Golden Eagle country here. As the morning drifts into the afternoon and the air becomes warmed thermal currents develop. These the Eagle takes advantage of and soars along effortlessly, sometimes at considerable height.

Continuing southwards along the metalled road you will pass by some habitations on your right and soon the track drops away giving an open view of the tree-covered flats of the upper glen. Creag na Caillich, the Hill of the Old Woman, stands sentinel at the head of the river flats and divides the glen. The main River Feshie disappears away to the left in its

Some Low Level Walks in Strathspey

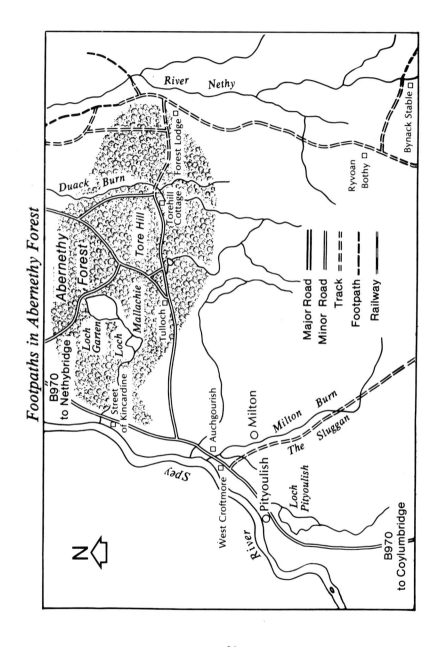

Footpaths in Abernethy Forest

River Nethy

Bynack Stable □

Ryvoan Bothy □

Forest Lodge □

Duack Burn

Torehill Cottage □

Abernethy Forest

Tore Hill

Mallachie

Tulloch □

Loch Garten

Loch

B970 to Nethybridge

Street of Kincardine □

Auchgourish □

Milton ○

Milton Burn

The Sluggan

Major Road
Minor Road
Track
Footpath
Railway

West Croftmore □

Pityoulish ○

Loch Pityoulish

Spey

River

B970 to Coylumbridge

N

Some Low Level Walks in Strathspey

steep-sided gorge with its public right-of-way to Deeside.

At this point another substantial wooden bridge crosses the river. Before descending the bank and crossing the bridge look for the low stone monument on a mound on the right of the road. This commemorates, as can be seen from the inscription, the 2nd World War use of the glen and its surrounding hills as battle training grounds.

Having crossed the river follow the track through the trees of the ancient forest. Notice the small enclosed area in which young trees have been planted, further attempts to restore the forest of the glen. The river flats, as can be seen from the vegetation, are very attractive as grazing grounds for the Red Deer. The enclosures give the young trees a chance to escape the browsing attention of the deer.

A short distance ahead now, and among the scattered trees on your left, is the Ruigh-aiteachain bothy, another of the welcome refuges for the Deeside-Speyside walkers, and others too. Whilst the bothy is kept in a weather-proof state, and provides a relative degree of comfort, the other buildings in its vicinity have not fared so well. A remarkably substantial chimney is all that remains of one of them. This chimney is what is left of the Landseer's chapel. That well-known animal painter of Victorian times was a frequent visitor here. By the ruins round about it is so obvious that people lived here in times past. Take, for instance, the rather unusual single trees here and there. The solitary, but old, Beech tree is certainly not part of the ancient forest.

At this juncture, and presumably you have had an exploratory wander from the bothy base, the track is now homewards. On the return journey there is a view of Glenfeshie Lodge on the other side of the river, sheltered in its trees from the winter storms.

Shortly before reaching Stronetoper you may cross the river by a substantial bridge at Achleum, a former croft. Continue downstream crossing the Glenfeshie estate boundary by the stile and follow the track uphill to Achlean croft where the public road from Feshiebridge ends. Continue down this quiet road to Feshiebridge.

As an alternative to starting this walk at Tolvah gate you may consider using Achlean as the starting point, an advantage being that it is possible to bring a car up the public road to that point.

No. 5   Tulloch Moor. Kincardine Church — Aundorach.
Map: Abernethy Forest. Distance: 6/8 miles.

Tulloch Moor is an area of moorland lying between the Kincardine Hills on the south and Abernethy Forest on the north and east with the

Some Low Level Walks in Strathspey

River Spey and the main road B.970 on the west. It is intersected by a very minor road of very mixed quality, but since this booklet is concerned with walking it is as well to leave any motor vehicle in a parking place as much will remain unobserved from the confines of a car. In any case, when on foot one acquires a greater flexibility in the choice of walks in an area such as this.

The walk starts where the unsignposted very minor road branches off to the east on the B.970 about halfway between Nethybridge and Coylumbridge. Near this road junction is Kincardine Church, very isolated but in many ways an interesting church. It has its origin in the 15th century, but like many buildings in the Highlands fell a victim to inter-clan strife as a result of which it was set on fire. It remained roofless until its restoration at the end of last century. Note the 'Leper's squint' in the east wall of the building. Through this slit lepers were able to take part in services without contaminating the other worshippers. Another interesting feature is the Laburnum tree just inside the churchyard gate. This undoubtedly is a tree of considerable antiquity and has lived through many centuries of Highland history.

To return to the Tulloch Moor track; there is a convenient car parking space on the right a short distance along the track. Continuing on foot it will be seen that here is a typical Strathspey moor. Heather is the dominant vegetation with boggy patches some of which are occupied by sheets of standing water. The typical Pine is notable by its absence. Here the Birch takes its place. This fact, I think, contributes to the special nature of Tulloch Moor. With its base of the typical glacial sand and gravels on which peat has accumulated over the centuries the drainage is poor. Farmland appears on the sloping ground bordering the foot of the Kincardine hills and continues eastwards until it merges with the slopes of Cairn Rynettin.

Naturally late Spring and early Summer are the favoured times for walking here. The patches of the yellow Bird's Foot Trefoil along the roadside add colour to the scene. Among the heather the small papery white flower of the Mountain Everlasting will be found, as will the white multi-petalled flower of the Chickweed Wintergreen, which is neither a chickweed, nor a wintergreen but is a member of the Primrose family. The Spring bird life is of special interest. The Black Grouse is regularly to be found here. It has its 'lek' grounds here where early on a Spring morning the cock birds gather and, with the Greyhens discreetly in the background, ritually display against each other. The drumming of the Snipe often fills the morning air. Skylarks and Meadow Pipits are prominent whilst the Whinchat occupies its song perch on the ranker heather. Ranging low

Some Low Level Walks in Strathspey

over the moorland the Short-eared Owl may be seen on its hunting expeditions. It is one of the day-time owls. The Merlin with its rapid dashing flight is another moorland hunter, taking the Meadow-pipit or simply the heather-feeding Emperor Moth. The Buzzard too is a regular visitor. Overhead the Osprey from nearby Loch Garten makes its feeding flight between its eyrie and Loch Pityoulish. The birchwoods have their own bird populations. Willow Warblers, Spotted Flycatchers and Redstarts are typical summering birds, together with the relatively resident Cole and Long-tailed Tits. The Redwing is a typical birchwood species and has been heard here during the breeding season. Also associated with the birchwood is the Redpoll. Their chittering flocks may be seen in the autumn.

A small lochan just off the track to the left can produce one or two duck species. Although well sheltered by the reedy fringe a Mallard or Teal may be seen. A Heron may rise from the edge and croak its way back towards its tree-top heronry in the Garten direction.

Two miles or so from the start the road becomes public and enters the fringes of Abernethy Forest. Tracks lead off right and left to the hillside farms. The Birches become more substantial trees and now have a slight mixture of Pines. The road now joins another public road at a 'T' junction. To the left the road leads to Loch Garten (1½ miles), to the right further into the fringes of the forest and eventually to Forest Lodge (3 miles) or Nethybridge. See Walk No. C.5. The 'T' junction is the return point.

No. 6 Kingussie — Ruthven Barracks — Ben Bhuidhe — Glentromie Lodge — Bhran Cottage — Return to Tromiebridge.
Map: Glen Tromie. Distance: 12 miles (max.)

Here is a walk, not strenuous, which uses in part the very ancient tracks through the Grampians between Badenoch and Atholl, between the Garry and the Spey. Here are tracks which in history have seen the passage of many peoples, kings and drovers, some in peace and some in war. Comyn's road, built by a Comyn, a name well steeped in the pre-Robert the Bruce history of Badenoch and Atholl, is believed to have its origins in the late 13th century. The Minigaig Pass was a later route originating perhaps in the 16th century. Whenever their origins there is little doubt that Ruthven Castle was either the start or finish of these tracks. The castle was the seat of the Comyn Lords of Badenoch, followed by the Wolf of Badenoch, then the Earl of Huntly, Chief of the Gordons. By the time the Ruthven Barracks were built in 1718 the General Wade's road over Drumochter had been built and the two tracks through the Grampians to Atholl became of less importance.

Some Low Level Walks in Strathspey

Walk in Glen Tromie

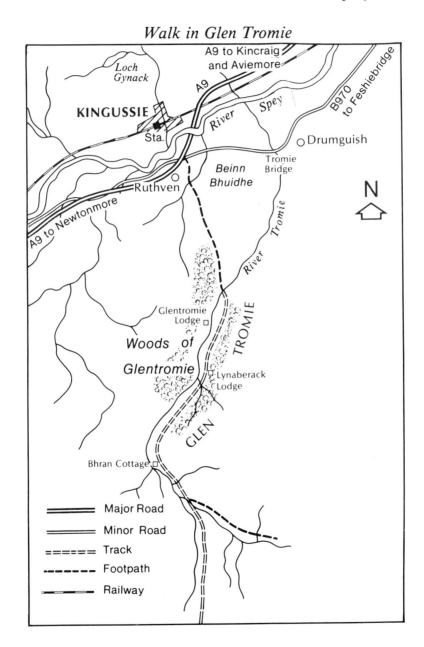

Some Low Level Walks in Strathspey

Our walk starts in Kingussie and by following the road to the River Spey, and passing under the new A.9 trunk road, Ruthven Barracks is soon reached. The Barracks, incidentally, were built on the site of the castle which had been destroyed in 1689 by a force under the Jacobite Viscount Dundee as a reprisal against the Duke of Gordon who supported the new King William. It is difficult to avoid references to the rich intricacies and intrigues of Scottish history when examining any Highland scene. The barracks themselves were built in 1718 to house government soldiers, the Redcoats, who had been sent to the Highlands after the 1715 Jacobite uprising.

Opposite the barracks and on the east side of the road a gate leads into the track which makes its way uphill alongside a field. The ruins of Brae Ruthven are reached, which were as recently as 1880, a typical highland clachan, and now consists of one small building used for farming purposes. There are numerous signs of former settlements in this area. Depopulation was inevitable when the harsh economics of the crofting life here were exchanged for regular work giving a low but regular wage with the coming of the railway to the Spey Valley in the 1870's.

The track, well defined, continues uphill passing on the left Beinn Bhuidhe, the 'yellow' hill. Shortly afterwards with the Birchwoods of Glen Tromie ahead over the heather moorland there is a choice of two tracks. One goes off right along the hillside in a southerly direction. This is the Comyn's Road. It continues along the hillside and in about three miles drops down to the River Tromie and joins the main glen road about one mile north of Bhran Cottage. As the track was descending to the river it passed Carn Pheigith, Peggy's Cairn. Its origin is vague but is believed to represent the grave of a suicide which occurred in the 14th century.

To return to the point where the tracks diverged; continue down to the birchwoods and join the road by Glentromie Lodge. Cross the bridge over the River Tromie and proceed right up the glen road. As a natural history scene the glen here with its birchwoods, Junipers, crags and river is very rich. From this aspect alone the walk is very rewarding. It is sheep grazing country; therefore it is Raven country. Peregrine Falcons and Golden Eagles may be seen high overhead. Buzzards, Sparrow Hawks, Merlins, and perhaps other raptors, may be encountered. In the summer small birds are very numerous in the woods, on the riverside and on the hillside moorland. Spotted and Pied Flycatchers, Redstarts, Redpolls and the ever-present Chaffinch are amongst the species which are otherwise too numerous to detail. The riverside has its usual quota of Sandpipers, Oystercatchers, Grey and Pied Wagtails, etc., the moorland its Whinchats, Wheatears, Meadow Pipits and Skylarks.

Some Low Level Walks in Strathspey

On continuing up the road towards Lynaberack notice the wayside wild flowers; Bird's Foot Trefoil, the common ground-hugging yellow flower, the Wild Thyme, Bearberry, and here and there amongst the richer grasses, the Yellow Mountain Pansy. Lynaberack, a new building, is a shooting lodge. The riverside meadows here contain a very attractive botanical display in the summer and are well worth examing. The Golden Plover, in its breeding plumage a very handsome bird, frequently feeds in these meadows.

Two miles or so further up the glen Bhran Cottage is reached. The trees of the glen have been left behind; the high-hilled moorland vista lies ahead dominated by the forbidding Gaick with its steep-sided glen. The name means the 'cleft'. In the cleft lies Loch an t-Seilich, the loch of the willows. Gaick Lodge lies beyond the loch. It is a lonely place. Yet, within the past 100 years the glen was well populated as will be assumed on the walk up from Glentromie Lodge. Ruins, or simply the foundations of houses, give indications of a substantial population. Lynaberack alone had six houses including the school for the glen children. Dailriach, a short distance from Bhran Cottage contains the foundations of a number of houses in the riverside meadows. Signs of earlier population are everywhere.

A mile beyond the cottage the road divides. The Minigaig Pass route continues uphill on its way to Blair Athol, while the road to the Gaick crosses the river and heads southwards into the great 'cleft'. If your time permits walk up to the loch. The lonely grandeur of the scene is excitingly impressive. It is deer country here and herds may be seen by the loch or on the hillsides.

The return journey is by the same route in reverse, but instead of crossing the bridge at Glentromie Lodge continue down the glen road to Killiehuntly and the main road. Turn left here for Kingussie.

Some Low Level Walks in Strathspey

GROUP C.

No. 1 Loch-an-Eilein/Coylumbridge/Whitewell to Loch Morlich via Iron Bridge.
Map: Rothiemurchus and Glenmore. Distance: 5/6 miles.

The alternative starting points for this walk are covered in Walk No. B.2. That route describes the journey as far as Piccadilly, the track junction entering the Lairig Ghru. We continue therefore from that point.

Our track leads on uphill and continues through the natural forest with all its interesting plant and bird life. Soon this forest starts to open out. The trees become more widespread. You have left behind the boundary of the National Nature Reserve and you are now on an estate footpath. On the right the forest is replaced by a fenced Forestry Commission plantation, and up on the side of Castle Hill may be seen Rothiemurchus Lodge, an army outdoor centre and hostel. In the near distance Loch Morlich now appears. The track is downhill and soon the Forestry Commission fence and stile is reached. Note the unusual gate for dogs.

You have now joined the private road which connects the Lodge with the main A.951 road at the west end of Loch Morlich. Again you are walking over gravelly, glacial moraines. The low hillock in front of you is a typical drumlin, a vast glacial deposit of sand and gravel. Now the road continues down over the tree-studded moorland, and having passed two wayside lochans crosses the River Luineag and joins the A.951.

If you wish to add another two miles or so to your journey you will find a track through the Glen More Forest Park a short distance back from the bridge. This track passes along the south side of Loch Morlich, through the forest and joins the main road about ½ mile beyond the caravan/camping area. However, walks in this forest park are mentioned in Group D.

No. 2 Loch Morlich — via the Sluggan — Milton — B.970 to Coylumbridge or Nethybridge.
Map: Ryvoan Pass and The Sluggan. Distance: 4 miles.

This is a walk mostly through the Queen's Forest of the Forestry Commission. It starts at a track, sign-posted The Sluggan, at the west end of Loch Morlich, on the forest side of the road. It continues through the forest for about 2½ miles, gradually climbing to reach the forest boundary

Some Low Level Walks in Strathspey

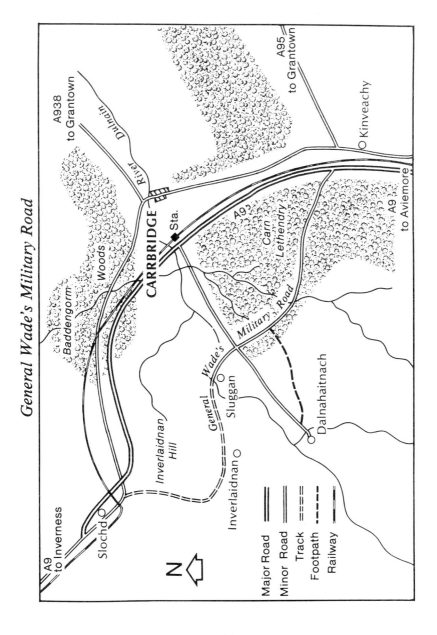

Some Low Level Walks in Strathspey

just north of Creag a' Ghreusaiche. Near the boundary is a large stone tablet commemorating the origin of the forest. Also near the boundary a road leads up to the left to the top of the Creag where the prominent T.V. relay mast is situated. The general features of the forest are described in Forestry Commission literature which is available at the Glen More Information Centre.

Having passed through the boundary gate the track is now downhill. On your right, and in a deep gorge, is the Milton Burn flowing northwards. Your surroundings have now undergone a change, a very marked change too. The plantations now give way to the natural forest of Birch, Juniper and Pine with the usual Blaeberry and Heather carpet. Birdlife is the same as in the other natural mixed open forests, and has already been described in other walks. The track continues to descend, passing Milton Cottage on your right, and enters farm land with its rough hedges of Gorse, Briars, etc. with banks of Broom resplendently yellow in June. Broom is a very natural component of the vegetation of these sandy, gravelly, glacial soils. The pass over which you have just walked was a glacial channel at one time.

The Corncrake, that fast-vanishing species from inland Scotland, but still commonly heard on the west coast rough grazings, has been heard in these pastures around you. Listen for it on a May evening. The birdlife is now of the distinctly farmland group. Even the Magpie may be seen here.

Soon the track reaches the main road, the B.970, on which you turn left for Coylumbridge or right for Nethybridge.

No. 3 Wade's Road — Sluggan Bridge — Carrbridge. Sluggan Bridge — Inverlaidnan Hill — Slochd.
Map: Wade's Road. Distance: 3½/6½ miles.

General Wade's Military Road is a familiar name on maps of the Highlands; even in the north of England the name Military Road is not unknown. These were largely the work of General Wade who, following the abortive Jacobite Rising of 1715 under the Old Pretender, 'James III and VIII', was given the task of opening up the Highlands by a system of roads to facilitate the movement of the government troops, the Redcoats. The government at that time had been very concerned over the initial successes of the Jacobites and realised that their inability to move the Redcoats rapidly, and from fixed garrisons, had contributed largely to these initial successes; hence the military roads. The one on which you are about to walk is a section of the road from Stirling to Inverness and includes the usable remains of a bridge over the River Dulnain which,

Some Low Level Walks in Strathspey

whilst not so spectacular as the Wade's Bridge over the Tay at Aberfeldy, is nevertheless a very gracefully attractive structure. The route itself is not so scenically spectacular as some others already described, but as you walk along it you are walking in the steps of Highland human history with all its bloodshed, miseries and hardship.

The track starts at a point on the B.1952 (the former A.9) about ½ mile North of its junction with the A.95, the Grantown-on-Spey and Elgin Road. A rough road, signposted 'Private — no unauthorised vehicles' leads off to the left among Pines and Birches and soon crosses the railway. The track continues over the new A.9 via two gates. Care is essential in crossing this road since it tends to generate high-speed traffic. The track continues uphill and keeping to the right passes through young Spruce plantations which fall away to the north. Below, and northwards, are the remains of old Pine forest which, at some relatively recent time, seems to have been ravaged by fire. The hill on the right in front is Carn Lethendry, and the farm is Lethendryveole. The view to the north over Carrbridge takes in a wide sweep of distant hills over the lower valley of the River Dulnain. As you approach the hill-top the ordered plantations give way to Birch and Juniper scrub, again with Heather and Blaeberry. Note how the bird life changes as you pass by the farm buildings and hedges. Yellow and Reed Buntings, and Greenfinches may be seen, typical birds of farmland country. Perhaps you may see a Blackcock, or the Greyhen, in the field adjoining the trees.

Soon the track starts falling away to the north-west, again with its vista of the gently rolling lower slopes of the Monadh Liath hills. In August these hills, like others, are vast extents of purple Heather. Immediately around you are new plantations of conifers well fenced in against the browsing of the deer.

A mile or so after having crossed the burn you reach a public road. At this point you may turn right and follow the road down to Carrbridge, a distance of about 2½ miles, but before doing so, cross the road and make your way down the track to the Sluggan Bridge. Then return to the road and to Carrbridge.

The track downhill to the River Dulnain provides a marked contrast to the scene through which you have just passed. Here you are in native forest of Pine, Birch and Juniper, a rich growth of vegetation, and because of its natural mixture, abounding in wildlife. The Roe Deer makes use of this woodland, and it is very much favoured by the Black Grouse, the 'edge of the woodland' grouse. The whole range of both summering and resident Speyside woodland birds can be found here. Crested Tits and Crossbills are common. The Redwing can be heard. Siskins, Tree-pipits,

Some Low Level Walks in Strathspey

Redstarts, and Spotted Flycatchers are usual species at the right time of the year. The tracks of the Roe Deer are to be seen on the softer edges of the road and on the many narrow but obvious tracks through the trees.

Soon you will come to the river, and there before you is the Sluggan Bridge and, despite its 250 years of existence, still fit for pedestrian use. Unfortunately, the ravages of the flood-prone Dulnain are taking their toll. For how many more years will its existence as a usable bridge continue without adequate conservation measures.

At this point a number of alternatives are at your choice. Firstly, take a casual wander up the river and notice how the river is forced by the steep banks to wind its way up a very tortuous course through the vast deposits of boulders, sand and gravel. Look out for Dippers, Sandpipers, Grey Wagtails, and the Ringed Plover with its particularly effective camouflage. The piping of the Oystercatcher is the feature of many Highland rivers. The Common Tern is a surprising bird to find so far up the river from the sea. The Golden Plover, a common bird of the high moorlands, comes down to feed in the riverside meadows in large numbers. Secondly, you may retrace your footsteps to the public road and continue downhill to Carrbridge. Thirdly, you may go on ahead having crossed the bridge. Wade's Road bears round to the left and follows along the south facing slope of Inverlaidnan Hill. Having continued for about 3 miles the track then crosses the railway and joins the old A.9 at the Slochd Cottages.

No. 4   Loch-an-Eilein – Loch Gamnha – Inshriach Bothy – Feshiebridge.
Map: Inshriach.   Distance: 6 miles.

This route may be regarded as a 'through' route or may be modified according to the needs of the walker to make it a 'there-and-back' walk.

The walk starts at the Loch-an-Eilein car park and follows the track round the east and south-east sides of the loch. The track is well described in the Nature Trail booklet issued by the Nature Conservancy Council. By the time you reach Loch Gamnha you will have joined the 'Thieves Road', Rathad nam Mearlach, a track used in times past by cattle raiders from Lochaber on their foraging journeys into the richer cattle lands of Moray. Passing the loch on its south side you now enter the area known as Inshriach. On the left are the Pine covered slopes of Creag Fiachlach and on the right, beyond the loch, the crags of Kennapole Hill, a place traditionally associated with the Wild Cat. The loch, although small, has a wildness of its own. It is the typically shallow loch of the glaciated plain with its boulders and muddy silt. In the reeds, during the breeding season,

Some Low Level Walks in Strathspey

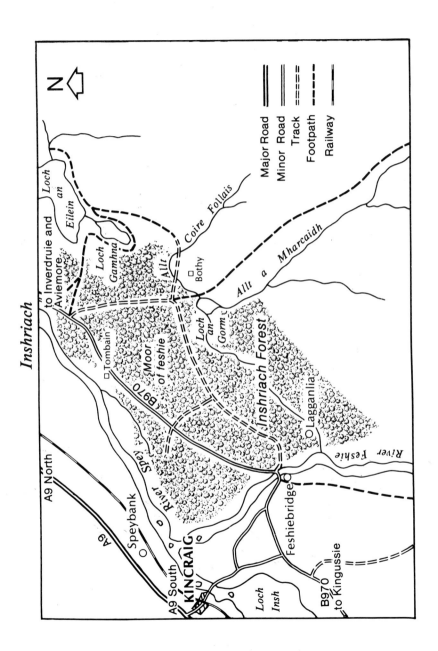

Some Low Level Walks in Strathspey

the Mallard and the Teal may be seen, but any waterfowl here tend to seek the concealment afforded by the reeds. A usual breeding bird is the Common Sandpiper, and the Greenshank has been seen using the muddy shore in its search for food.

Continue along the well-defined moorland track for about a mile. The track then fords the Allt Coire Follais and continues down to an area of old Pine forest. On the right, between the track and the well-ordered forestry plantation, lies an extent of wet, marshy ground into which the Follais burn empties itself. This is good Teal country, whilst Meadow Pipits and Skylarks abound. The relatively large day-flying moths, the Emperor and the Northern Eggar, may be seen flying low over the heather particularly in May and June. Later in the summer the large dragonfly, the Aeshna, is very prominent, as is the common Blue Damselfly, both flying swiftly and low over the marshy ground.

Now the path drops gently in the beautifully attractive glade of old, or even ancient, Pines and in a small grassy clearing is the Inshriach Bothy. Here you see the typical natural forest. The natural mixture of Pine, Birch and Juniper is obvious. Notice, too, the magnificent old Rowan tree on the edge of the bothy clearing. Richly laden with its berries in September it provides a welcome port-of-call for the southward bound flocks of migratory Thrushes from Northern Europe as they follow the Spey Valley route to the winter shelter of Southern Britain.

As you continue along the track, now in a north-westerly direction, observe on the trackside the small Birch seedlings in the shelter of the heathery banks. Soon you cross a sleeper bridge and on your left is Lochan Gorm, or rather, what is left of it. Apart from a few small stretches of water, what used to be a loch is now an extent of reeds and peaty mud with ancient Pine roots showing on the surface. Typical bog vegetation is to be seen here. Note the abundance of Butterwort, with its basal rosette of bright green leaves, the Cross-leaved heath in flower in July, the Cotton-grass and Lousewort. Later the yellow spiked Bog Asphodel adds colour to the scene. Bird life is numerous and varied here. The old woodland has Crested Tits and Siskins; its Tree-pipits, Redstarts and innumerable Chaffinches. The water and marshy area has its few ducks, mainly Mallard. The Common Sandpiper nests here. Undoubtedly it is an exceedingly attractive area for many species of birds. Patience and observation without disturbance, could be rewarding.

As you continue gently uphill towards the forestry plantation fence, which is also the National Nature Reserve boundary, stop and look back at the hill face which you have left behind. Note how rich is the natural Pine cover, and how well defined is the uphill limit of growth. This is an

Some Low Level Walks in Strathspey

example of the highest natural tree line in Britain. Note how rounded are the hill tops in contrast with the craggy corries of Loch Einich. The corrie in front of you is the Coire a' Mharcaidh. The high hill in the background is Sgoran Dhu Mor which, on its other side, overlooks Loch Einich. These hills are deceptively high. Even Geal-charn, the hill on the right of the corrie, is over 3000 feet high. The corrie itself is a gathering ground for the Red Deer, which with the aid of glasses may be seen in the corrie from summer onwards. Note also the large stone block on the ridge on the hill on the left, Creag Dhubh. This is the Argyll Stone, or in its gaelic name, Clach Mhic Cailein. Its association with the Duke of Argyll may, or may not, rest on the fact, but amongst the various stories is the suggestion that it dates from the winter of 1644 when the Duke of Montrose, a fervant supporter of Charles I, raided the Highlands to raise support for the royal cause and deal rigorously with the Covenanters who opposed the king. Assisted by a small army of Irishmen and Highlanders from the Isles he achieved remarkable success. Having ravaged Aberdeen and the North-east he set off westwards over the Deeside hills and glens towards Strathspey. The Duke of Argyll with his Covenanters' army was waiting in Strathspey to intercept Montrose. The Argyll Stone is said to be the spot from which the Duke espied Montrose and his men. But to no avail; Montrose succeeded in making his way westwards and raided the lands of the Campbells of whom Argyll was the Chief. Apart from this association with the Campbells, as the translation of the name implies, the stone is simply a mass of disintegrating granite caused by its exposure to wind. The wind blasts pieces of granite grit on to the stone and the continual abrasive action of the grit results in the blocks of granite being worn down, a slow but inevitable process. Similar blocks, but on a wider scale, may be seen on Bynack More and Ben Avon on the eastern edge of the Cairngorms.

Continue now to the fence and the stile crossing into the forestry plantation. But before doing so you may find it attractive to walk along to the Allt Mharcaidh by way of a diversion. Turn left at the fence and a short distance along the track another track leads off to the left and wanders down to the burn which emerges from Lochan Gorm. A footbridge crosses the burn. Continue by the track over the boulder strewn ground towards the trees. The river, with its many channels and boulders, is on your right and a new plantation lies further over. Continue along and uphill into the open forest as far as you wish. Return now by the same track to the stile and the N.C.C. stone sign. Cross the stile and follow the forest road. By keeping to the main track you will reach the main road, the B.970, at the Forestry Commission cottages. However,

Some Low Level Walks in Strathspey

about ½ mile short of the road another main track branches, slightly back to the left. Follow this for a mile and you will arrive at Feshiebridge. Alternatively, you may simply wish to back-track from the stile and return to Loch-an-Eilein.

No. 5 Glen More – Ryvoan Pass – Forest Ledge – Nethybridge.
Map: Abernethy Forest. Distance: 11 miles.

The Glen More to Ryvoan Bothy and Forest Lodge routes are fully described in Walk B.1. On reaching Forest Lodge from the Ryvoan track there is a choice of route to Nethybridge, both of which involve walks through the Abernethy Forest. First, on reaching the motor road turn right and follow the road towards Forest Lodge. Passing by the cottage continue down towards the bridge. Take the track to the left before the bridge and passing by the fenced-in garden continue through the gate. The track skirts the river and climbs through the forest to a point where there are extensive views over the Dorback Moor to the east.

The track then descends and joins the alternative route where it continues to Dell Lodge. There it joins the public road which drops down to Nethybridge.

The alternative route is to turn left when leaving the Ryvoan track and walking along the estate private motor road for about ½ mile another branches off to the right and leads down through the forest to join the other track to Nethybridge.

No. 6 Easter Lynwilg – Allt-na-Criche – 'Burmah' Road – Caggan Bridge – Inverlaidnan – Carrbridge (Alternative diversion via Wade's Road to Kinveachy).
Map: Lynwilg to Carrbridge. Distance: 11 to 13 miles.

This is not entirely a 'Low Level' walk since the first three miles, on a good estate road, is distinctly uphill rising to a height of about 600 metres from a starting base of approximately 230 metres. From the highest point on the track it is more or less downhill for the remainder of the walk. Nevertheless on the uphill walk the breath-recovering stops do provide the walker with the opportunity of admiring the vast panorama of the Cairngorms from an entirely fresh point of view. The route starts at Easter Lynwilg on the A.9 about two miles south of Aviemore and three miles north of Kincraig. At that point a private road branches off in a north-westerly direction on the north-east side of the burn, the Allt-na-Criche. Continue up this road for about half a mile. On your

43

Some Low Level Walks in Strathspey

Footpath from Lynwilg to Carrbridge

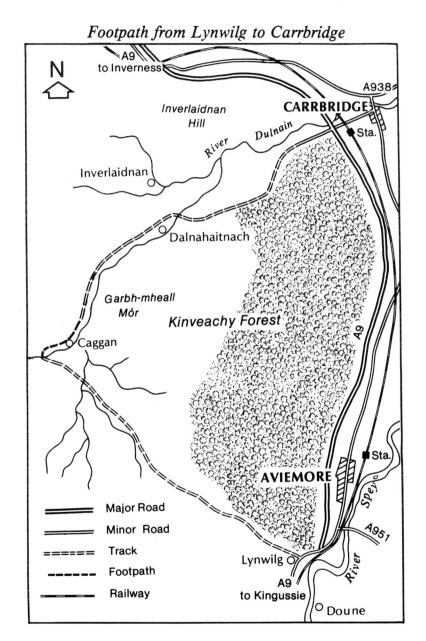

N

A9
to Inverness

Inverlaidnan
Hill

CARRBRIDGE

A938

River Dulnain

Sta.

Inverlaidnan

Dalnahaitnach

Garbh-mheall
Mór

Kinveachy Forest

A9

Caggan

Sta.

AVIEMORE

Spey

A951

Lynwilg

River

A9
to Kingussie

Doune

	Major Road
	Minor Road
======	Track
- - - - -	Footpath
	Railway

Some Low Level Walks in Strathspey

right is the Birch-clad south westerly side of Craigellachie hill. At the track junction fork right and having crossed the gate continue uphill. It is of interest to note the isolated Scots Pines standing in very exposed and inhospitable situations among the heather, yet surviving, but although there is a profusion of cones around the base of these trees there are no signs of natural regeneration. This may be attributed to the fact that the heather moorland through which the track climbs is Red Deer territory – 'Deer Forest'. Still continuing uphill with the burn now far down below on your left a more profuse growth of trees, mainly Birch, may be seen in the shelter of the gorge. Before the track bends round the shoulder of the hill on your right take the opportunity of studying the mountain scene behind you. In the foreground the Duke of Gordon monument on Kinrara Hill is now well below the point you have reached. Walk No. C.4 gives the names of some of the prominent summits you can see. In late spring and summer the typical hill moorland bird species are well represented here. Skylarks and Meadow Pipits are common. The Ring Ousel may be heard in the river gorges. The Curlew is well distributed on the heather moor. Overhead a passing Peregrine Falcon may be observed whilst at moorland level its relative the Merlin is well at home. The Red Grouse is the most prominent moorland bird for this is also Grouse moor.

Continue up the main track ignoring any lesser tracks which may go off right or left and having crossed two minor burns the moorland starts to level off. A top-of-the-world feeling pervades the scene and soon you will observe that the streamlets alongside the track are flowing in the same direction as you are walking. The downhill section of the route has started. Soon the Cairngorms are out of sight and there in front of you is the great expanse of the Monadh Liath mountains – the Grey mountains. There are no spectacular summits to be seen but the uniformity of altitudes is impressive. On the downhill journey, and having passed the wooden bothy, the heather and peat structures of the grouse butts will be seen. A further mile ahead will bring into view the wide valley of the River Dulnain with the Caggan Bridge at the foot of the hill. Having crossed the bridge turn right but before continuing spend a while examining the gorge of the river here. The rock structures over which you have walked are the Moine Schists, a very ancient rock series containing a mixture of rock types, Sandstones, Limestones and other sedimentary rocks, with Quartzites etc. all radically changed by earth forces. In the gorge of the river here may be seen the rocks from which the surrounding hills are made. Some are resistant, some are softer, hence the gorge through which the river runs. Riverside birdlife is particularly interesting here in the late spring and summer. The Goosander, a saw-

Some Low Level Walks in Strathspey

billed fish eating duck, nests here. The Grey Wagtail is its near neighbour. The Dipper will be seen on a rock projecting above the surface of the water. The Common Sandpiper will pipe its riverside journey up through the bridge, as will the Oystercatcher, a relatively numerous bird in the highlands.

The route continues by a well defined track, or you may make your own way on the riverside. You will pass the crofts of Caggan and Eil. Crofting has gone on here until relatively recent times as can be seen from the condition of the respective buildings. The river terraces do tend to produce fairly fertile land, but the river Dulnain means in English the 'place of the flooding'. Floods are common. Life for the crofter would have consisted of a series of adversities. Hence the abandonment of the crofts. The great Moray Floods of August 1829 are worth mentioning at this point. On the night of the 27/28th five inches of rain fell having been brought in on an unprecedented north-east wind. The torrential consequences were disastrous for the whole of the Findhorn, Dulnain and Spey Valleys. This vast rainfall over the area through which you have walked completely washed out the whole valley and all its bridges, crofts, cattle and crops. The toll in human life must have been serious since no prior warnings were available in those days.

The track downstream passes through remnants of the ancient Caledonian Pine forest with its mixture of Birch and Junipers, Rowan and Aspen. More extensive Pine woodland will be seen on the other side of the river. You may observe Red Deer sheltering in those trees. As you approach the more open moorland the former croft of Dalnahatnaich will be seen on the east side of the river. Here the river flood plain widens. The remains of the old wooden bridge will be seen. Here rejoin the main track on the edge of the moorland and continue to its junction with the track which branches off northwards to the Slochd. Among the Pine trees at the junction will be seen a granite monument erected to the memory of Iain Beag MacAndra who, it is believed, lived sometime in the 17th century. The legend concerning this worthy, but diminutive character related to his skill with the longbow and the routing of a band of cattle raiders from Lochaber. The raiders had, on a previous occasion, ravaged the Dulnain area but had been routed by the local crofters. They returned seeking revenge but beyond the name of the crofter, MacAndra, who had been responsible for the rout, had no idea of the appearance of their intended victim. The raiders duly arrived at the croft, forced their way in and were confronted by the guidwife and what looked like a small small young lad sitting huddled round the fire. They demanded to see MacAndra. The guidwife threw a plaid over the 'young' lad by the fireside

Some Low Level Walks in Strathspey

and sent him off up the hill to bring his 'father' down to the house. The 'young' lad, on leaving the house quickly climbed into the nearest pine tree with his longbow and picked off the raiders one by one as they anxiously came out of the house to see why the 'laddie' was taking so long to find his 'father'. There was no further trouble from the Lochaber cattle raiders; hence the monument.

A track is discernible down the bank towards the river. Follow this downstream by the edge of the Pinewoods, through the gorse and juniper scrub and soon you will see the farmland of Inverlaidnan. The rough meadows here are favourite feeding grounds for Golden Plover, Dunlins, Lapwings and Oystercatchers. A short distance ahead is the new bridge over the river. Cross here, right up to the public road which leads to Carrbridge, 3 miles ahead. A diversion route via the Wade's Road is described in Walk No. C.3.

A DEAL WITH DEATH

CRESCENT CITY WOLF PACK BOOK FOUR

CARRIE PULKINEN

ABERDEENSHIRE LIBRARIES

2114613

This is a work of fiction. Names, characters, places, and incidents are either the product of the author's imagination or are used fictitiously, and any resemblance to actual persons living or dead, business establishments, events, or locales, is entirely coincidental.

A Deal with Death

COPYRIGHT © 2019 by Carrie Pulkinen

All rights reserved. No part of this book may be used or reproduced in any manner whatsoever without written permission of the author except in the case of brief quotations embodied in critical articles or reviews.

Contact Information: www.CarriePulkinen.com

Edited by Victoria Miller
Cover Art by Victoria Miller

First Edition, 2019
ISBN: 978-0-9998436-6-6